Glenna Luschei

Edited by Rena Ferro

Victory Garden

Poems

University of New Mexico Press
Albuquerque

ISBN 978-0-8263-6452-4 (paper)
ISBN 978-0-8263-6453-1 (e-book)

Library of Congress Control Number: 2022946091

Founded in 1889, the University of New Mexico sits on the traditional homelands of the Pueblo of Sandia. The original peoples of New Mexico—Pueblo, Navajo, and Apache—since time immemorial have deep connections to the land and have made significant contributions to the broader community statewide. We honor the land itself and those who remain stewards of this land throughout the generations and also acknowledge our committed relationship to Indigenous peoples. We gratefully recognize our history.

Cover photograph adapted from photograph by Dawid Zawila on Unsplash.
Cover Design by Felicia Cedillos
Interior Design by Isaac Morris
Composed in Garamond 10.5 | 13

In memory of my
daughter Linda Glenn Luschei

Hail me Diogenes, O stranger, and pass by.
In my nineteenth year the darkness drew me down
And ah the sweet sun.

—from the Palatine Anthology

CONTENTS

Part I. THREE STRANGE ANGELS

Pilgrimage	1
The Yellow Blanket	3
The West	4
Orderly	5
Abuela	6
Return to the Great Plains	7
I Ate the Heart	8
Victory Garden	9
My Father's Work	11
Grass Skirt	12
Scrap Metal	13
Twirling	14
Living as My Parents Did	15
Sick Room Story	16
Barn Stormers	18
Nuclear War Is Nuclear Family	19
The Century Plant	20
One More Day	21
Bullet for the Werewolf	22
Observance	23

Part II. LOVE OF PILGRIMAGE

Spring the World Over   27
Mourning Doves   28
Safe Passage for Bill   29
First Date in Pioneers Park   30
Forgive Me   31
Obsession   32
Water Bearer   33
Daughters-In-Law   34
My Cat, the Shah of Iran   36
Cricket   37
Canada Goose   38
The Year of the Cock   39
Summer through the Southwest   40
Riddle   41
Ghost Photography   42
Calving   43
From Willa to Edith   44
Taking Communion at the Border   45
Hombre   46
Prison Count   47
Possum   48
Dawn   49
Meeting Moriarty   50
Five Billion   51
The Fabulous Planet Uranus   52
I Want to Come Back   53

Acknowledgments   55

Part I

"Who is the knocking?
What is the knocking at the door in the night?
It is somebody who wants to do us harm?

No, no, it is the three strange angels. Admit them, admit them."

—D. H. Lawrence

Pilgrimage

Ear to radio, tracking the fire, I remember the photograph
of Navajo Code Talkers wearing headphones in Iwo Jima.
They transmitted Marine Code Diné, a language the enemy
had never heard, could not break.

All night I stay awake clinging to bulletins
until firemen pound on my door, hand me a mask.
"Go now."
Through swirling ash and cinder they lead me to my car.

I race away from flame, dodge flying branches.
From my rearview mirror, the fire tunnels down the mountain
toward my ranch.

I fly in safety to low-slung Albuquerque,
air so clean it stings.

On to Chimayó, *El Santuario*
and the holy dirt. "The miracles don't come from statues. It's the dirt.
Open up the floor," the Pueblo people told the padres, and they did.

This is where the suffering gather soil for healing,
where the faithful join the procession to throw away their crutches.
I came here to light the candles, once with breast cancer,
another time with failure of the heart.

I live on and long in gratitude, remember the Death March soldiers
walking sixty-five miles after they surrendered Manilla. They prayed
and promised each other, "If we are saved, we will march each year
to Chimayó."

Still they walk to *El Santuario* from Albuquerque, from Clovis, from Carlsbad. They walk for the holy dirt.

They march sixty-five miles in White Sands.

After I smudge dirt on my forehead, I light a candle and kneel. Pray my house is safe from fire.

The Yellow Blanket

I

Skulls and crossbones
flag everything today.
The wage of sin is death.
Shivering, I enter the Cuban ICU.
In Spanish, the nurse says
a woman died today and since
her family did not pick up her things
I could have her blanket.

II

Let me mend the nets
net the night
only one wish
to stay alive.
Hauling up the water yoke
I've come back from the dead.

The West

I

In delirium I returned to the West,
which commences with the Missouri, heart
of the waterways
where Sacajawea, papoose on her back,
plunged into the current to retrieve the talking papers
of Chief Redhead,
Meriwether Lewis. He sketched each plant and herb
that Sacajawea picked to bring them health. From there
the Voyage of Discovery found its path across the West.
Sacajawea delivered her son, Laughing Boy, on my birthday.

II

Let me inherit from them who plowed the Missouri
and from John Neihardt who ordered me,
"Run wild with the sandbars and rapids."
From Willa Cather who said, "The musk of the River
tears the heart out of me, that place where
they still call me Willie."
She traveled to a land she loved
even more: New Mexico, with its Rio Grande.
She took me with her.

Orderly

"Vaya al misa. Dar unas almas a los pobres.
Take care of your affairs. Stay home . . ."

—Don Quijote's housekeeper

I who preferred folly to correctness, loved madness,
learned the virtue in routine
from the young intern who saved my life.

The orderly entered the ICU, light beaming from his brow,
like the young Jesus entering the Temple.
One by one, he methodically took our vitals.
When he came to my cot he pulled the pills from his pockets.
"Here is your prescription, belonged to my father.
He's dying, wants you to have them."

Enough to get me back home.

My son scoured every *farmácia* in Matanzas for those pills,
telephoned Havana. No luck.

The trick is you never know when ordinary might burst
into grace as when Jesus spoke with the woman
at the well, or when he said, matter-of-factly, "Let him
who is without guilt cast the first stone."

Abuela

I bit the dust in Matanzas
like the Spanish fleet
the Indigenous Cubans destroyed.

I bit the dust in Matanzas
where all mornings unfold alike.
The nurse dabs me awake with cold
water from the mountain stream.
She leaves the liter bottle stamped
with the troll to last all day.
All Cubans drink the same fairy-tale water.

All afternoons sleep.

Abuela tunes up, "*Ay Dios mio ayúdame.*"
Second day I have entered her litany.
She chants, "*Ella es Norteamericana y habla espanol.*"
By the time she winds down
the nurse brings us rice and a drumstick.

Late afternoon the TV clicks on.
Children march in the streets.
Abuela naps.

Evening at last. Another drumstick.
The nurses retire
and I creep out to the heavenly unlocked balcony.

Night goes on.
The fiesta convertibles and stray dogs
pass each other in the street.

Return to the Great Plains

First trip back since the hospital,
I pray to feel at home on the Great
Plains, but I am barely at home with the living,
pretending I know how to register,
sign my name.

In a month the lilacs will broadcast
their perfume. For now, the leaves pitch
hands in prayer.

Open: save me, save me.

The highway wiped out our living room,
bricked me in until you heard my heart,
and led me stumbling over stones.

My Indian guide on the Niobrara signals I can make it.
I camp with Lewis and Clark on the lake
where I learned to swim,
visit Sacajawea on her keelboat.
The herbs she collects will cure me, Grandmother's ointment.
I must not have died because I feel cold.
Alive, I slip my hand through your arm,
an icicle that makes you jump.

"Don't you walk with a stick?"
Yes, but I crave the warmth of a sister,
as I walked with Grandma and her witching rod.
She knew I would find and bear water,
first to love me for my wildness.

No one else let chickens roost on my cast-iron bed.
She gave me her diamond, knew I was a traveler
and would need ready cash, left me her Roads
to California quilt and linen tablecloth.

I Ate the Heart

"The Japanese bombed Pearl Harbor."
I heard the news from the hallway,
my parents crouching in front of the radio.

Everything changed.

Then my father wore an air-raid helmet and carried a flash-
light door to door every night.
At last, "All clear."

Once, by accident, I turned on the hallway light
then collapsed, waiting for the bomb to fall,
sure I had killed my family, wiped out the whole town.

At the post office, Uncle Sam pointed at me,
but no Zeros made it to Sioux City.

All winter we saved gas-rationing coupons
to drive to our grandparents' farm, away from war.
Grandmother ushered us into hallways of peace.

She hoarded her coupons for baking cherry pie,
too sour without sugar, served platters
of fryers. I ate the heart.

My parents laughed and chased us in tag.
We swam in the Republican River,
pumped well water for washing our hair.

I hated to go back to the war.
On the drive home we picked up a sailor in uniform.
He held the baby in his lap.

Victory Garden

"Let the field be joyful, and all that is therein:
then shall all the trees of the wood rejoice."

—Psalm 96:12

After the sun went down and the fireflies came out,
we kicked off our one good pair of rationed shoes
and went barefoot. Carrying rakes and baskets we sang
in the joyful fields Pastor spoke about in his sermons,
moved like ghost dancers in the corn.

First came Great-Grandfather, wounded twice
in Vicksburg, who returned then to his soddie,
served in the Nebraska legislature. At the picnic table
he read the family Bible by kerosene lantern.

While we worked, Grandfather sat in the Adirondack,
played his violin, "Tenting Tonight."
He knew the names of the constellations,
and Homer and Thucydides, his prayers for the parents
of the Athenian dead, a speech too hard to bear.

Father dug potatoes and I scrambled
to throw them in the bucket;
on vacation, the garden his vacation.
He didn't have to go to this war, but
above the Victrola we hung a picture of him
wearing a tall expedition hat from the First War.
He said every soldier got a blanket to belt across his chest.

The widows too joined in, one pulling a baby carriage.
A woman who rented the upstairs apartment came
to help hoe around the tomatoes. While her husband
was on bivouac, she pasted Shirley Temple scrapbooks.
Sometimes I climbed the pine tree to peer into their apartment.
I wanted to glimpse married life.
I wanted to grow up.

My Father's Work

Our teacher asked what our fathers did.
When friends said, "WPA,"
I asked my dad, "What's the WPA?"
To explain, he took me to our post office. A man on a stepladder
painted tunnels of wheat on the wall and farmers with fat legs.
The man climbed down, handed me a paintbrush.

"The wheat needs a little more ochre," he said.
I had never heard *ochre*.
The most beautiful word,
and I fell in love with the smell of paint,

and the murals of Coit Tower in San Francisco.
Cowboys and orange-pickers painted on walls
meant escape from poverty, Dad said.
It meant soup for the first grade.
I paid a quarter for soup and a nickel to see Roy Rogers
at the Saturday picture show.

A friend gave us a loaf of bread she cooked
with bacon grease. My mom's bread was the best.
We shared it with men who came looking for work.
She baked bread in coffee cans. The loaves came up like mushrooms
cooling on the windowsill.

Decades later, I heard my father's secrets:
"He bought me my first suit of clothes."
"He took me off the street."
"He sent a truckload of coal."

What I loved most about the Depression were the Indian Head pennies
my father gave us to put on the railroad tracks.

Grass Skirt

When couples parked to spoon on the banks of the Missouri, they sighted German U-boats tunneling beneath the River.

Onawa, Iowa, Halloween, 1943

Mother walked us to school that day. We lugged the Winesaps for apple bobbing. Not enough syrup to make popcorn balls like last year. Cold out. In our jacket pockets we carried war-bond books.

I carried my grass skirt, too, for show and tell. When I wrote my soldier I confessed my longing for a grass skirt like the ones they showed in the war movies. Army censors marked out his return address, but I knew where he was stationed because he also sent me a shell bracelet that spelled out Figi. Mother said my grass skirt smelled like seaweed, but I loved it.

As we passed Mrs. Wilson's house we remembered when a soldier and Father Murphy stood on the porch. Mrs. Wilson shrieked, "Oh no, not my boy." My sister and I ran to her. Neighbors gathered to help her back into the house.

When we got to school, we read on the blackboard, "Help finance a Jeep." "Jeep" was easy. We had to sound out "finance." That day our war-bond money went for the Jeep in honor of our school. In class I read my poem about my grandfather's long johns on the clothesline leaping like kangaroos. Margaret Ann asked if she could hear it again.

I didn't know how to write poems about the war, only kangaroos, Figi Islanders, and Athena riding Pegasus.

Tricks or treats at night. Pumpkin candle for a light. I wore my grass skirt over pajama bottoms. Sad at Mrs. Wilson's house. Her three blue stars in the window; now the gold one. She smiled and handed out Hershey bars. Wherever did she get them? On the way home, snow surprised us. We walked over ice, covered in white. We followed in someone's footprints, maybe the ghost of a soldier looking for home.

Scrap Metal

I was eight years old and wanted to win
the scrap-metal drive.
I asked father to dispatch the lumberyard truck.
After Shorty drove back with the mattress springs and dumped them
on the playground, my excitement began to build.

The trucks came back again trembling into the schoolyard
with cast-off pumps and windmill blades from old farms.
My brothers donated
glistening tinfoil bars.
Wait! Is that my grandfather's cast-iron bed?
Would he sleep on the floor? I don't remember.

After Spam sandwiches and grape pop, the superintendent called us
to the auditorium. He announced my name and pinned the sterling
victory pin, Dot-Dot-Dot-Dash in Morse Code, to my flannel shirt.
He saluted me and I saluted back.

I learned a lot. My family would do anything
to help me, especially Grandfather, who gave up his bed.
The senior boys in the auditorium returned to graduate in uniform.
One had a purple heart.

Twirling

How dressing up in red, white, and blue crepe paper
and twirling a baton would beat the Nazi's escaped me,
but I was cast and my parents came to the gym
to watch my stiff-armed performance:

the only girl who couldn't flip the baton with her toe,
to send it on a dazzling figure eight
cascading down her back.

It was a cold walk home in my crepe-paper costume.
No one spoke. The next week Mother
enrolled me in tap-dancing.

Living as My Parents Did

I wanted to please my parents.
Being a fighter pilot was out,

I just wanted to live as my parents did.
They took blankets to people sleeping in boxcars.

Mother taught us and the neighborhood kids Spanish at the desks
Father brought home from an abandoned schoolhouse.

They sent us to Mexico and we fell in love
with the country and the people.
One day I moved to El Paso. On to Albuquerque.

Sick Room Story

You name it, we had it.

Flu, measles, strep throat, earaches, a mastoid operation
not counting the time I ran my arm through the washing
machine wringer, elbow broken, two places.

We landed in the Sick Room
bureau crowded with cod liver oil bottles, my sister's adenoids
floating in a jar, the portrait of General MacArthur.

Mother rang up grandparents in Nebraska.
They came to Iowa by train carrying liniments, snake oil, and the two
Rhode Island Reds I raised from chicks last summer
on the farm.

Fresh eggs, a good start.

They bundled us in Grandmother's quilts and told us stories.
Grandfather told about crossing the prairie in a covered wagon,
two thousand dollars sewn in the mattress,
played Shenandoah on his mandolin: "Cross the Wide Missouri."
When the Sioux raided, Grandmother hid her birthday cake in the barn.
They took a hog instead.

While we napped she went down
to the riverbank to dig turmeric and gather peppermint
for our sore throats.

Then told the tale, "Sacajawea picked herbs from her keelboat,
and Lewis recorded them in his journal.
When Lewis dropped it into the river,
she went in after it, papoose and all.

On my tenth birthday Father built me an easel.
Mother gave me paints, a brush, and a notebook for my poems.

Father bought a sunlamp for the Sick Room.
A six-foot intruder, it glowed and ticked, did the trick.

> We got well, listened
> to MacArthur's farewell on the radio,
> bought an automatic washing machine.

Barn Stormers

"Buy your Victory Garden seeds here!"
I hawked them from door to door.
"Radishes and lettuce, a nickel a packet."
I made enough to buy a hand warmer for my cousin,
Planted my patch at the farm.

Father told how cold it got in the trenches.
In World War II my cousin flew a B34,
still got cold in the air.
When he flew over the barn, he dipped his wings.

Nuclear War Is Nuclear Family

Manhattan Project, not the Easter Parade,
rather the bomb that blew up our lives.
We all exploded in that Big Boy blast
the forties, the fifties, the infinities lost forever.

For the nuclear family builds the nuclear bomb.
The mother of three everyone beats up on.
He goes to pieces Christmas Eve and socks her.
She doesn't ask why. She knows she has to be up
the next morning while children tear open presents.

We don't talk about it or report the beatings.
They continue. It is the great Manhattan Project,
secrecy in our lives.

Scientists met in Los Alamos, New Mexico,
beneath the elms. Why can't the peacemakers meet
in tranquil New Mexico,
beneath the elms, beneath the aspen,
knowing the aspen is all one body as we are?

The Century Plant

The road scared
me but Tom
on furlough slammed
on brakes anyway
when he saw
the Century Plant
flowering great big
(blooming so majestically)
from the side.

We might slide
and wreck but
worth the danger
to see what
I can be
at one hundred.

One More Day

Waiting me out
Death watches me grow plump enough for a tasty morsel,
children captured by the witch.
I stick my fingers out through the bars for Death to calculate
how they have rounded.
A cruel game He plays with me, but hey!
It's one more day. I'm still alive.

What a clanging celebration in my heart
when the first rays pierce the sky and holler, "Rise."
Or let me doze.

Remembering the photographs of the liberated Americans
at Java: their ribs and collarbones stick out.
They grin at the indescribable pain
of being alive and free.

Bullet for the Werewolf

When you were a young athlete
I dreamed I held your fine shrouded body
as Mary embraced her son in the Pietá.

The men in our family encircled us.
Some condemned you.
In the fullness of time,
what crime do they suspect
you would commit?

Uncle Wade anointed me.
Aviator from World War I, he built
his plane from a Sears Roebuck
kit sent out by train. He flew
a Dr. Brewster to Kansas,
slept in the cockpit at night
as cattle tried to eat the plane for banana oil.

My father, Scorpio like you,
wept.
Why does death
run that deeply in our family?
I accept my children
will die before me.

The dream foretold betrayal.
I know the silver bullet
for the werewolf would enter my heart.

Observance

"If ye break faith with us who die
we shall not sleep, though poppies grow
in Flanders fields."

—John McCrae

Twenty-nine-thousand American crosses bear witness
at the Normandy cemetery. I walk the fields
along the Rouen where farmers in their stone
houses sheltered American paratroopers.
Here the red flower, the *coquelicot*, covers the land.

As I pick a bouquet of poppies
a woman tells me I must singe the roots
so they will raise their heads.
That's us, our roots singed for survival.
    I pray the dead will sleep,
    keep faith with them.

Part II

LOVE OF PILGRIMAGE

"When in April the sweet showers fall
and pierce the drought of March to the root, and all.
The veins are bathed in liquor of such power,
as brings about the engendering of the flower. . . .
Then people love to take a pilgrimage."

—Geoffrey Chaucer, *The Canterbury Tales*, Prologue

Spring the World Over

For J. L.

"Have a good one,"
the clerk at Trader Joe's says.
He loads the tulips and the hyacinth into my cart.
Doesn't the Holy Koran instruct us if we have five dollars,
spend one on hyacinths?
Maybe I overdid it in my vow to make this day
ecstatic, not routine.
Inspired by my mailbox
overflowing with eastern euphoria,
I vowed to make every day Spring.

A friend from Michigan saw a bass jump.
Another in Upstate New York
longed for the afternoon, only a week in the future,
when he could sit in his hammock
with a beagle in his lap.

Humble celebrations, yes,
but mine is more modest.
I give thanks for the good one the clerk
offers.

All I want is one more good one
when my heart surprises me,
waking me up to its pumping,
like an accordion in Tuscany.

Mourning Doves

When Bill died we both turned into doves.
I call them the Bill and Glenna doves.
They splash water out of the bath.
We were like that. Anything for a laugh.

When Bill's a little late,
I don't fret. We'll meet up, fly together.

Zenaida Macroura

Safe Passage for Bill

Take care of my husband, Osiris.
He, too, was a sailor
always seasick.

Keep the waves gentle for him.

First Date in Pioneers Park

First date in Pioneers Park you brought a softball and a mitt,
taught me to catch.

A triumph since the captain chose me last in PE.
Had there been girls' soccer like my granddaughter plays
I could have become an athlete.

But the fifties scored girls on how fast
they married and had babies. I did well. I had a litter,
strong, beautiful, and athletic like you.

I knew they would be smart because in education class
I gave IQ tests to my boyfriends. You scored the highest.

Years and years. I loved the ones when you were a diplomat.
We sat in the opera box next to the president of Colombia.

Graduate school. They called it Ph.t.: Putting hubby through.
We were divorced and no more maids.

Yoga, Tai Chi. I became an athlete on my own
while our children starred.

When I needed funds to educate them, you said,
"I contributed my genes." Yeah. Sure. You were smart,
but not that smart.

Years and years. You told my family if it weren't for you,
they would have to pay someone to take care of me. Yeah. Sure.
I started my own business. You asked me for a loan. I said, "Yes".

When I remember those days tossing softball, you squinting
into the sun, my heart opens out to you like a glove.

Forgive Me

They were delicious
so sweet
and so cold

—WCW

I know why William Carlos Williams ate those plums:
so sweet, so cold.
I nearly shoplifted them.
So hungry, so pregnant
that summer in the Black Hills.

The flurry of letters to the cabin on Bluebell Route
chronicles my misery
sixty-five years ago. He would not buy me plums.

My father wrote that sometimes women needed expensive food
when they were expecting (his first grandchild).
He enclosed a check.

My mother-in-law wrote that canned food also carries vitamins
a pregnant woman needs. No need for fresh fruit.

So hungry, so pregnant.

I foresaw a lifetime of canned-fruit cocktails.
Even if I got all the cherries it would not make up
for those plums so tart they made you shiver.

So hungry.

Was it then or later I knew I had married the wrong man?
I wanted that creature who lived with me in the Garden of Eden,
the one who gave me the apple.

Obsession

1.
He was my first love,
but without sense to move on,
sticks around in dreams.

2.
In my daydreams too
he has something to offer
from fifty years past.

3.
Many bad choices.
Too late to do it over.
His hair, widow's peak.

4.
The main problem was
we were both too young to know
this was once in life.

5.
My therapist said,
"That person haunting your dreams
is really yourself."

Water Bearer

My name with two N's
carries the Nile in it
to irrigate Egypt's seed.

Let me be Water Bearer.
I may not pass this way again.

I end with the A,
the raven that cleans the carcass.
Lions go a long time
between kills.

Panthera leo

Daughters-in-Law

My daughter-in-law doesn't look
twice before she jumps on a bus blasting merengue.
She trusts the *chiva* will butt her where she needs to carry on
the revolution.
She doesn't look like me.
Why should she with my hair that resembles Grey Poupon,
even the gray part?

Her hair is black as a raven's wing and her eyes click like castanets.
She treats boys with fierceness, not fear,
offers a gang member tattooed and pierced a ride
home through rival territory.
Kindness and bravery: her watchwords.
She forced the bus driver swerving through Colombian mountains
to stop to let the passengers knock on a hut to use the bathroom.
The driver wanted to shoot her down, but she was a quicker draw.

Back in the US she nearly performed a citizen's arrest
on the waiter slow to serve a Mexican family.
Best of all, she inspires my grandchildren to treat me, their abuela,
second only to la Virgin de Guadalupe.

What miracle did I perform to merit a daughter-in-law like this,
plus the Sicilian one who serves struffoli for Christmas?
That one tells me some day she'll take me to her native Sicily.
Arm in arm we'll walk through the piazza in our black skirts,
shiv at the garter.

I did the right thing by my sons, though when Dominica and I
drive through Skid Row on the way to the Mission, I flinch
when she offers my son's overcoat to a man freezing on the corner.
She says, "He needs it more."

I'd like to return to Sicily where in antiquity
my own kind, the Cyclops worked as smithies.
People identify me by my third eye.

I can see it all now.
After my long life, I need those women worse.

My Cat, the Shah of Iran

Along with the celadon vases for my mantle
and the dolphin sculpture,
my lover left me his cat, the Shah.
Raised from that feral kitten,
le chat orange, he prospered into the imperious
Shah of Iran.

He reclines on my chest,
stills my heartbeat,
nods as I weave a new tale, like Scheherazade,
that will grant us one more day.

Cricket

Cricket, when you blew
your whistle at two a.m.
I had to get up
to the tapping of the Hahn
at five.
I wanted to step outside,
jam on my thongs, and stamp.

Then I thought
what a gift you've got with your improve.
You just blast it out.
I have to beg most poets
to speak up.

Acheta domestica

Canada Goose

We called him Wellington:
his long black boots.
He knocked on our door
with his beak.

He took off in the dark
flight of geese
over the lake.
We expect him back.
Next time goslings?

Branta canadenis

Year of the Cock

The rooster is Christ
announcing the dawn.

—New Mexico Proverb

Flame Feather,
you were my first familiar.
Grandmother let me bring you in
to roost on my cast-iron bed.

I saved you from Grandfather's hatchet
until you attacked me.
Still, I stand up for beauty: the rooster.

Gallus gallus

Summer through the Southwest

My favorite site:
not the Grand Canyon,
Pike's Peak,
but the trough at the Socorro
Rest Stop,
water to the brim.
Thirsty livestock.

Bos Taurus
Equus ferus caballus

Riddle

What is the purpose of a fence?
To keep the peacock safe
from lions lurking in the grass.

To protect her from the kangaroo
loose
in the outback.

But what of a peacock tamed?
If she is maimed,
can she endeavor to show her true color?

What is the purpose of the nest?
To give the flying flock a rest
when they alight to drink.

Purpose of the empty cage?
To mourn the songbirds now extinct.
To answer the riddle: sadness, rage.

Pavo cristatus

Ghost Photography

New Year's Eve I'm alone for a new beginning, and I resolve to hike
that ancient path, the Franklin Trail. Fog swirls around me.
I make out the light of my house below.
How I ever stumbled back I do not know, but when I drag
myself to my door, it's locked.

Where's my key? I don't remember leaving
the light on, but I brush past the camellias. Through the window
the kerosene lamp flickers.
There they are, sepia lit: Bill's grandmother, whose gravesite I will inhabit,
and his grandfather, Bernard Franklin, who laid out
that Franklin Trail that got me lost.

That stylish young woman at the piano would be Aunt
Betty. She talked her father into changing the garage
of the old Victorian into a darkroom. She roamed the Southwest
with her camera. She and I loved the territorial houses
of Edward Curtis. I preserve her photographs and her library.

I'm the photographer now, pointing my lens at them,
black hood over my head. This will be a still life
since all are dead.

I know that handsome man in uniform standing in the corner.
Always shy, he was my Bill, then and forever.
He told me how before the Japanese left for Manzanar
they came to say farewell and to thank the Franklins for letting them use
the Sulphur bath.

I take their pictures, dread finding myself locked out
all night. When I try the door, it opens and I move to greet my guests.
But the room is bare, and I wake up alone in bed.

Calving

Poseidon sent the whale, Cetus, to destroy
the shores of ancient Greece.
Scientists call Tahlequah's care for her dead calf unprecedented,
but isn't it natural to carry the dead with us, lift them up as she did,
all eight hundred pounds of her baby, only rising to take a breath, lifting?

How can the orcas survive when we net their fish, plow boats
into their mating grounds? Can this pod, with only one live birth, go on?

Our calves die of addiction, bullets, transmission of love. We lift them up,
keep them floating with us.

II
On our last Mother's Day I visited hospice. You asked me
to feed you. After, I wheeled you under the purple jacaranda trees.

You told me the nurse loved to brush your flaxen hair.
"God gave me a mane." You handed me the brush and I took your curls in hand.
"Tomorrow is my quality-of-life conference." I kept on brushing.
You had to decide.

Aphrodite, you knew my beautiful daughter and her vanity.
Lend her your brush, your mirror.

From Willa to Edith

1.

In Taos when a lady asked me how Mable Dodge
Lujan could marry an Indian, I answered,
"How could she not?"

I met Tony, antelope to her macaw, who leaped
their shrouded path.

Now, Edith, egret to my desert, how could I not?

2.

Indians call the crescent
"moon holding water." In Italy when you were sick
I bathed your forehead with linen.

3.

D. H. Lawrence told me I had eyes in the front
of my head. Like an owl, I could turn my sight
around. He called me all-knowing. He told me
Americans are lone wolves.

He did not know I have you, your owl's hoot.

4.

Meet me, ancient Puye. Dwell with me in ledges.
Wind jangles the keys, Yeast
rising in the moon. Wind jangles to sleep.

Taking Communion at the Border

"He then made soft clay and shaped it into twelve doves. . . .
Jesus clapped his hands and shouted to the doves:
'Be off, fly away, and remember me, you who are now alive!"

High in the Santa Cruz Mountains, a miracle.
It snowed.
Whole doves of snow
swerved into my windshield wipers.

Jesus said when he broke the clay,
"Doves fly away."

Ah, let them fly South as birds do.

Children crossing the border one by one.

The migrant and his child drowned on the banks
of the Rio Grande. Shooting victims in El Paso.

Since Methodists have but two sacraments,
communion and baptism, let me be baptized
with immigrants in the Rio Grande.

Let me soar with the doves
to celebrate with the faithful,
take my portion of the tortilla,
pass my Sierra cup through the fence.

Hombre

The morning I fired him,
sent him back to New Mexico
Tedlock said, "Don't be like me;
I went through life
with one hand tied behind my back."
That evening when he packed
he showed me his elegant pistol
that slept by his head.
"It's a good one," he said.

He took along his dog,
adopted in the few days he stayed here.
I hired that hombre to help me out.
Instead he brought a pack of troubles.
Is that what he meant?
I never knew.
Only that we were two of a kind.

Prison Count

I was only your teacher of verse,
but you chose me to walk you down that vale.
I prayed to be worthy.

You couched your medals and keys into the paper,
all you had. You left me your white sage

for bathing. I beseeched the shell
in the sweat lodge to anneal your brokenness.

From the yard PA:
"The count is clear.
The institution count is clear."
One less skin tomorrow.

We held tight,
walked in matching steps.

Rattle of the Chumash shaman.
"May your transgression find clemency."

You winked at me. I bowed to you, rendered
you to Exit.

No chair.
Lights did not dim.
You chose Oxycodin.
Everyone does.

Possum

When we lived in that redwood house
built 'round an oak tree,
the children gathered at the kitchen table.
custody battles complete.
I stepped outside. I couldn't take the merriment.
Their giddy relief
scraped down my spine.

The branch next to me
held a mother possum, four
joeys on her back,
my own four jostling inside the house.
I knew her babies tiny as honeybees,
twenty to a litter.
On birth they crawled into her pouch.

Four of them on my back,
I barely provided.
I lived in the wilderness of marsupials,
my pouch their safe house.

I learned what it meant to scavenge as an animal,
to know the slaughter hour,
to be born white.

How did I survive? We got through.
I go back inside, bring them bowls of popcorn.

Dawn

My cat jumps on the bed, ears wet,
outside rain. He makes his way
over my body's Appalachia, one damp paw at a time,

shedding feathers from his wren encounter.
Awake now, I wonder if I shake
my mountainous frame I can find the bird, help
him escape.

The cat's asleep now. Perhaps dreaming of summer
and the blue lizard he will present to me.
Too early, too cold, the flapping against the pain!

Meeting Moriarty

Your language sounds like the water in which you tried to drown me
at Pie de la Cuesta. Always water, always children, always in Spanish,
your ghost comes to haunt me, to taunt me.
You taught me duende, told me I was a fighter worthy
of your wrath, told me my heart would get me.

Fifty-two years ago they sent a diver out after me.
The waves tossed me, but I could still see my son on the shore.
Thrashing, I watched him getting smaller and smaller,
I couldn't drown.
I had to drive him to Little League ten years later
in a town where we had not yet lived.
I gave that swimmer my last hundred pesos, sodden, hidden in my bra.

Next time on the Rio Grande,
birth of a daughter in El Paso, deep vein thrombosis.
I ran the household from a wheelchair. I had cases to solve.
You're playing with me, Moriarty. You wanted to save me for yourself.

I should have known we would meet in Cuba,
when I bit the dust in Matanzas. The doctor said I would die if I got on that plane.
One week in hospital, my son flew me home first class.
Your ghost loved that, Moriarty. If only I could wait fifty-two more years,
I know you'd give me one more scare.

Five Billion

Every human is entitled to five billion heartbeats.

Because they sense I'm near death,
or maybe because they love me,
they treat my arrival at the writers' group
as an occasion.

They say, "Thank you for taking the time,"
understand I know the value of taking minutes.
I offer a shorthand of my allotted five billion heartbeats.
No more, no less.

I have to make time,
cast a sculpture, blow it like glass in the furnace of hell, shape it.
I have to create that fusion of time and mass.
If I smash it as I broke the glass starfish,
I may hear the bardos, the sea girls singing.

Each to each
for glass may not be recovered.
Impermanence is the law.

I return to rationing as we did during
the war when we sent butter to soldiers to keep them hardy.

Waste not, want not, they warned during the Depression.
So I have to make time count. One two five billion!

I loved those days of wasting time,
the most luxuriant lie that our lives will last forever.
Days of sleeping through the alarm.
Today I hear the metronome's *tick, tick, tick.*

One two five billion!

The Fabulous Planet Uranus

for my birthday February 11
Like me, Uranus takes eighty-four years to circle the sun.
We're just now winding up, off to a rocky start
on to the next orbit. I won't last that ride.
We're stocking up on provisions anyway.

Like me, Uranus lies sideways on its axis.
I feel fortunate to be singled out
for this quirky ride. I don't mind sharing my birthday
with others. Thomas Edison, for one, also intent

on incandescence, and Burt Reynolds.
Uranus, cold, blue, and windy, you are the God
of the sky. You are the reason I skate on ice.

I Want to Come Back

I want to come back with a murder
of crows lifting our feet through fescue grass.

I want to come back in the Mesozoic
where murderers nest in the Cycad tree.
We survivors of the fit pick Jurassic
fleas off the back of the Stegosaurus.

Stegosaurus armatus

Acknowledgments

The author would like to thank the editors of the following magazines for first publishing some of the poems in this book:

Rare Feathers: Poems of Birds and Art: "Riddle"
Pembroke Magazine: "Spring the World Over"
Spillway Magazine: "Taking Communion at the Border"
The Carpinteria Arts Center, *Top 100 Artists* Exhibition: "My Father's Work"